ESCAPE FROM TOMORROW

Sereta Lanning

A PACEMAKER BESTELLERS™ BOOK

FEARON·PITMAN PUBLISHERS, INC.
Belmont, California

Series Director: Tom Belina
Designer: Richard Kharibian
Cover and illustrations: Dick Cole

ISBN—0—8224—5258—3

Library of Congress Catalog Card Number: 77-75948

Printed in the United States of America.

1. 9 8 7 6 5 4 3 2 1

CONTENTS

CHAPTER **1**

THE EXPERIMENT

As he drove along in his car, Ben Daley felt happy.

He was happy because today was his last day at work. Tomorrow he would begin a new life. Tomorrow he would begin to do what he had always wanted to do.

Ben was going to live a simple life in the country.

He was going to live on a farm. There was a small house on the farm. There were fruit trees near the house. Ben planned to grow his own vegetables to eat.

He would keep some chickens. From them he would get eggs. He would also have some cows. They would give him milk.

He began to sing as he drove along.

Soon he came to the scientific laboratory where he worked.

He parked his car. He got out and went inside the laboratory.

"Good morning, Ben," a man said to him. He was about 50 years old, with white hair. His name was Jim Becker.

"Good morning, Jim," Ben said. "How are you on this great morning?"

"I'm fine, Ben. Just fine. But I am sorry to see you leave. Are you sure you won't change your mind and stay here?"

Ben smiled. He shook his head.

"Well, that's too bad," Jim Becker said. "I really hate to see you go."

"You can come and visit me sometime," Ben said. "My farm is only ten miles from here. I'll let you feed my chickens."

"Are you going to live all alone out there on your farm?" Becker asked.

"Yes. Just me and the chickens. And, of course, the cows."

"That doesn't sound like the kind of life I'd like," Becker said. "But never mind about that. Let's get to work."

He walked into a room that was full of test tubes. Ben followed him.

Both men put on white coats.

"Well," Ben said, "here we go again. One more time. I wonder if we will be able to make our experiment work today."

"There is only one way to find out," Jim Becker said. "Let's try it."

Becker picked up a test tube. He took it to the sink to fill it with water.

"What if we do learn how to make a new kind of water?" Ben said. "What good will it do?"

"I don't really know yet," Becker answered. "Not for sure, I mean. But all kinds of good things could come out of it. We will try some experiments. Who knows what will happen?"

Ben looked at Becker. But Becker wasn't looking at him. Ben felt funny. Jim Becker's words rang in his ears. *Who knows what will happen?* Well, they would soon find out, Ben decided.

Becker filled the test tube in his hand with water from the sink. Then he put several drops of a green liquid into the water.

"Take this," he said. He gave the test tube to Ben. "Heat it up, will you?"

Ben held the test tube over a small fire. Several minutes went by. Nothing happened to the water in the test tube.

"The water still looks the same to me," Ben said. "It isn't going to work, Jim."

"Don't worry," Jim Becker said. "I'm not finished yet. Here—try this." He gave Ben a little bottle. In the bottle was some blue liquid. It was very thick.

"Liquid X-23?" Ben asked. "Do you think that will do it?"

"Add two drops of Liquid X-23 to the water in the test tube," Becker said. "Let's see what happens."

Ben did as he was told. "What now?"

Jim Becker didn't answer him for a minute. He was looking at the water in the test tube. "Add another drop," he said.

Ben put a third drop of the blue liquid into the test tube.

As the two men watched, the water in the test tube changed. Slowly, it began to change its color. It wasn't green now. It turned to brown. It looked a lot like mud.

"It isn't working," Ben said.

"Let's start over," Becker said. He took the test tube from Ben and put it away. Then he took a clean test tube and filled it with water from the sink.

"I have an idea," Ben said.

"What is it?"

"Why not try just *one* drop of Liquid X-23? And some Hydronium." He picked up a little jar. Inside the jar was some dust. The dust was the color of gold. It was Hydronium.

"OK," Becker said. "Let's do it your way this time. Give it a try."

Ben put one drop of the blue Liquid X-23 in the test tube.

He held the test tube over the fire. When it was hot, he let some of the gold Hydronium fall into the test tube.

"Jim," Ben said. "Look!"

Jim Becker looked down at the test tube. Now there were bubbles in the water inside it.

Becker started to say something. But Ben held up his hand to stop him.

Ben put some more gold dust in the test tube.

Now there were a lot more bubbles in the water. Then white smoke began to come out of the test tube.

"Maybe this is it!" Ben said. "Maybe *this* time we have really done it!"

"Yes, maybe we have," Becker said. "I hope so. Give me that other empty bottle."

Ben picked up the empty bottle Becker wanted. He gave it to him. Becker put the water that was in the test tube into the empty bottle. Then he set the bottle down.

Bubbles filled the bottle. The water began to get thick. It changed color again. Now it was red—as red as blood.

Ben picked up the bottle and held it up to the light. "It looks thick enough now," he said. "Let's see what it feels like."

"Be careful!" Becker said. "Don't touch that water yet. Try it first on one of our white rats."

"OK," Ben said.

Becker went over to a box in the corner. He took a white rat out of the box. "Here," he said to Ben. "Try the water on this rat first."

Ben took the rat from Becker. He held it in his hand. He let a drop of the red water fall on the rat.

Almost at once, the rat began to change. As it did, it made little sounds. They sounded like little screams.

"Drop the rat!" Becker yelled at Ben.

Ben dropped the rat to the floor. Both men watched as the rat slowly turned into red jelly.

"That one drop of red water killed the rat," Ben said. "Why, Jim? Do you know?"

Jim Becker was looking at the rat. "I'm not sure," he said. "The red water seems to have changed the water in the body of the rat. It changed it into water just like itself."

"Do you know what that means?" Ben said. "It could do the same thing to the water in a person's body."

"Don't worry," Becker said. "It can't hurt us if we don't touch it."

"I'll tell you the truth, Jim. I'm very worried about that new water we just made."

"Nothing will happen. Not if we are careful." Becker reached for the bottle.

His foot slipped on the red jelly that had once been the rat. He fell against the sink. When he did so, he knocked the bottle over.

All the red water ran into the sink.

"Stop it!" Ben yelled. He was about to try to catch the red water. Then he remembered what it would do to him. It would turn him into jelly if he touched it.

He stood there and watched the red water. It ran down the drain. A minute later, it was all gone.

"Well, that's the end of it," Becker said.

"It's just as well," Ben added. "We should never have made it in the first place."

"But how is science going to learn new things if we don't experiment?" Becker said.

"I can't answer that," Ben said. "But I think there may be some things science should leave alone."

Ben washed the spot of red jelly that had been the rat down the drain.

CHAPTER **2**

RAIN

Two weeks later, Ben was at work on his farm. He had forgotten the red water. He was living the simple country life he had always wanted to live.

It was near the end of October. Soon it would be November.

Ben gave some food to his chickens. Then he milked his cows. He looked up at the sky. Looks like rain, he thought.

He walked back to his house and went inside. A minute later, someone knocked on his door. He went to the door and opened it.

"Hello," he said to the man who stood outside on the steps.

There was a girl with the man.

"Good morning," she said to Ben. "I thought we should come over and meet our new neighbor. My name is Carol Crane. This is my father. His name is Gus."

"I'm Ben Daley," Ben said with a smile. He shook hands with Gus. "Please call me Ben. Since we are neighbors now, we might as well be friends, too."

"That's fine with me, Ben," Gus said.

Ben hoped that it would be fine with Carol, too. She was very nice-looking. She had green eyes. Her hair was light brown. She had a nice warm smile.

Just then, they heard a bark outside the front door.

"That must be King," Carol said. "King is our dog."

"I guess he is looking for you," she said to her father. She turned to Ben and said, "King really loves my father. The two of them are the very best of friends."

Ben went to the door and opened it.

A big black dog ran into the room. It ran over to Gus and jumped up on him.

"Hello there, King," Gus said. He put his arms around the dog. It gave another bark.

"I'll make some coffee for us," Ben said. He went into the kitchen.

When he came back, he gave a piece of meat to King. He gave some coffee to Carol and to Gus. He also gave them some cake.

As they drank their coffee and ate their cake, it began to rain.

Gus Crane looked out the front window. "It's really coming down hard," he said. "Just like it did the day before yesterday."

"If it's raining this hard in town," Carol said, "there may be more trouble."

"Trouble?" Ben said. "Was there some kind of trouble in town?"

"Yes," Carol said. "There was. We read about it in the paper."

"What kind of trouble?" Ben asked.

"It happened over near that scientific laboratory in town," Gus said.

"I used to work there," Ben said. "What happened?"

"Well," Gus said, "the sewers were full of water because of the heavy rain. A lot of water spilled out of the sewers."

"That doesn't sound like very big trouble," Ben said.

"Oh, but it was bad," Carol said. "Because the water wasn't like real water."

Ben put down his cup of coffee. "What *was* the water like?" he asked.

"It was like jelly," Gus said. "The paper said it was almost as thick as jelly."

"And it was red," Carol said. "The paper said that the water was really very strange. It turned all the plants and flowers that it touched into jelly."

"There was something more, too," Gus said.

"What?" Ben asked.

"When the rain touched that red water, the rain changed. *It* turned into red water, too."

Ben looked out the window. Outside the rain still fell.

Should he tell Carol and her father that he had helped to make the red water? He decided not to. First, he wanted to find out more about what was going on. And see if there was anything he could do about it.

CHAPTER **3**

THE RIVER

After Carol and Gus had gone home, Ben picked up the telephone. He called the number of the laboratory.

There was no answer.

He hung up the phone and went out to his car. He drove to the laboratory as fast as he could. When he got there, he parked his car. He went to the door of the laboratory. There was a big sign on the door. It said:

CLOSED

The sign was a surprise to Ben. At first, he didn't know what to do next. But then he got back into his car and drove to a candy store. He used the telephone in the store to call Jim Becker at home.

The telephone rang only once and then Becker answered it.

"Jim," Ben said. "It's me."

"Ben?"

"Yes. I was at the laboratory but it's closed. Can I come over to your house? I want to talk to you about that red water we made in our experiment," Ben said.

"OK. Come on over to the house."

Ben left the candy store. He got in his car and drove to Jim Becker's house. He parked his car and went up and knocked on the door.

Becker opened the door. "Come on in, Ben," he said.

Once inside the house, Becker said, "Sit down, Ben."

"I heard what happened the day before yesterday," Ben said. "I mean when the heavy rain fell. I heard that the rain turned into red water like the stuff we made."

"That's right. It did."

"What I want to know," Ben said, "is what is going to happen next."

"I'm not really sure," Becker said. "But I do have some ideas. I believe the red water we made can grow. When it touches other water, the other water turns into red water. It can even change rain water into water like itself."

"Then we are in real trouble," Ben said. "People can't drink that red water. It would kill them—turn them into red jelly. If that red water gets into rivers and lakes, it will change them, too."

"That's right," Becker said. "It will. Someone has to find a way to stop it. If the red water isn't stopped, it could change all the water all over the world."

"And it will," Ben said, "if it ever gets to the ocean. People all over the world will die. They need water to live. And they can't drink—or even touch—this new water."

"I wish I knew how to stop it," Becker said. "But I don't. No one knows how to stop it."

Ben said, "I heard that the water even turned plants and flowers into red jelly. Is that true?"

"I'm afraid it is true," Becker said.

Ben got up. He went to the window. He looked up at the sky. There was no sign of rain. He turned back to Becker.

"We never should have made that new water," he said.

"Yes, you're right about that," Becker said.

Ben sat down. He began to think.

After several minutes, he said, "I think I had better come back to the laboratory to work. I want to help you with your experiments. After all, I helped to make that red water. It's up to me to help you try to stop it."

Becker shook his head. "No good."

"What do you mean?"

"I mean that you can't come back to the laboratory to work."

"Why not?" Ben asked.

"Because the government knows about what happened at the laboratory. I mean about the red water that we made. They told me to close down the laboratory. They won't let me do any more experiments—of any kind."

"I see," Ben said. "So that leaves me out, doesn't it?"

"Yes, Ben, I'm afraid it does."

Just then the telephone rang.

Becker reached out and picked it up. "Hello."

He listened for several minutes. Then he hung up.

"That was one of the government men," he told Ben. "He went out to check the water in the river south of town."

"The sewers here in town empty into that river, don't they?" Ben said.

"They do," Becker said. "The government man told me that the river now has a lot of red water in it. But that's not all he said."

Ben waited for him to go on. He was almost afraid to hear what Becker would say next.

Becker said, "The government man said that he saw dead fish in the river. The red water killed them. It turned them into red jelly."

Ben said, "That river runs right into the ocean a few miles away."

"It does," Becker said. "And you know what that means."

Ben said, "We must stop that red water. I mean before it gets to the ocean. But *how* can we stop it?"

Becker shook his head. He looked down at his desk. "I don't know how. No one knows how," he said.

Suddenly, Ben thought of his cows.

He stood up. "I've got to go," he said. "I've got to get home fast."

"Why?" Becker asked him.

"Because my cows drink water from the river. If they drink it now, it will kill them."

He ran out of Jim Becker's home.

As he drove along the streets of the town, he saw Carol. She was at the bus stop. He stopped his car.

"Can I take you home?" he asked her.

"Thank you," she said, giving Ben a warm smile. "I was waiting for the bus. But I would much rather ride home with you."

"Get in," Ben said.

Carol looked at him as they drove along. "Is something wrong, Ben?"

He told her about the red water. He told her what he had just learned in Becker's office.

"Oh, no!" she said when Ben finished speaking. "What are we going to do? What is going to happen to us?"

"We have to find a way to stop the water in time," Ben said. "Or we will all die."

When they got to Carol's farm, Ben stopped the car. "I'll talk to you later," he said. "I've got to go and check on my cows. I've got to keep them away from the river."

"I'll go with you," Carol said. "Maybe I can be of some help."

They drove over to Ben's farm. Both of them got out of the car and ran to the river.

"Look!" Ben said. "We didn't get here in time." He pointed.

There was a pile of red jelly by the side of the river. Next to it was a second pile.

"That's all that is left of two of my cows," Ben said. "They drank some of that red water."

"And it killed them," Carol said. "That's an ugly way to die."

"No, it isn't," Ben said. "And that water will kill more animals if we don't stop it."

"Not only animals," Carol said in a low voice. "It could kill people."

"Yes," Ben said. "It could. It could kill every living thing on earth."

CHAPTER 4
FENCED IN

Several days later, the army came to town. They had been called to fight the red water.

They set up their camp beside the river. Part of their camp was on Ben Daley's farm. He went down to talk to the soldiers.

"Do you think you can stop it?" he asked a soldier. "The whole river is almost all filled with red water."

"We don't know if we can," the soldier said. "But we sure are going to try."

"What do you plan to do?" Ben asked.

The soldier pointed to a truck near them. "See all that stuff on that truck? First of all, we are going to try that."

"What is that stuff?" Ben asked.

It looked to him like a big pile of wire.

"We are going to build a fence," the soldier said. "We will build it on both sides of the river. Once the fence is up, no more animals will die. The fence will keep them away from the water. They will be safe then."

"That sounds like a good idea," Ben said. "But what about the water itself? What are you going to do about it?"

"We were just told to build the fence," the soldier said. "That's all I know."

Some other soldiers came and said they were ready to start work.

"I'll see you later," the soldier said to Ben.

"Wait a minute," Ben said. "I want to help. This is my farm, you know."

The soldier looked at Ben. He smiled. "OK. I guess you can help us. Why not? I mean, we welcome any help we can get. What's your name?"

"Ben Daley."

"OK. Come on then, Ben. Let's get to work."

Ben followed the soldier down to the river. The soldier gave him a shovel. "You can dig holes for the fence posts with this shovel," the soldier said. "Start right here."

The soldier left. Ben heard him giving orders to the other soldiers. The other soldiers began to take all the stuff from the trucks.

An hour later, Ben stopped his work. His back was stiff. So were his arms. He had not worked so hard in years. But he didn't mind. He was glad to do it. He knew he had to stop the water. He had to try to save the land—and the animals and people.

He began to dig another hole for another fence post.

Behind him, soldiers put wood posts in the holes. Other soldiers nailed wire to the posts to make the fence.

Ben worked hard. He was so busy that he didn't hear someone call his name. The person called his name a second time. He looked up.

It was Carol.

He waved to her.

When she got to where he was, she said, "Did you join the army?"

"Not really," he said and gave a laugh. "I'm just helping out here."

"That fence doesn't look too strong," Carol said. "There is, I think, another problem, too. I don't want to cause trouble. But that fence should go several inches into the ground. Then it should be covered with dirt."

"I don't see why," Ben said.

"The reason is simple," Carol said. "If you don't put the wire down into the ground, animals can get under it. They will dig their way under it."

Ben thought about what she had said. He decided that she was right.

"I'll be right back," he said. He went over to the soldier he had talked with before. He told the man what Carol had said.

"My orders are to build the fence like this," the soldier said. "So this is how I'm going to build it."

An hour later, the fence was up.

The soldiers got into their trucks. The trucks drove away.

Carol turned to Ben. "The fence might save the animals," she said. "But it won't keep the red water away from the ocean."

"No, it won't," Ben said.

They looked down at the river. The red water was moving slowly toward the ocean—inch by inch. It kept changing the rest of the water it touched into water like itself. With each passing minute there was more of it.

"What the soldiers just did doesn't help very much," Carol said.

"Well, I guess they did their best," Ben said.

Carol turned. "There is someone coming," she said. "Trucks are coming."

Ben saw the trucks coming. "More soldiers?"

"No," Carol said. "Those men in the trucks aren't soldiers. They have work clothes on. I wonder who they are."

The trucks stopped beside Carol and Ben. A lot of men got out of the trucks.

"Hello," Ben said to one of the men. "Are you here to—?"

The man said, "The government sent us. We have a plan to stop that red water."

"What kind of plan?" Carol asked the man.

"I will tell you in a minute," the man said. He went to the men who had come with him. He gave them orders.

The men began to take a big machine off one of the trucks.

The man came back to Carol and Ben.

He said, "Do you see that big machine?"

Without waiting for them to answer, he said, "That big baby should do the job."

"What job?" Ben asked the man.

"It will pump the red water out of the river. Then it will heat up the water. The water will just dry up. That will be the end of it."

Carol looked at Ben. "Maybe," she said to him in a whisper. "But I have a feeling that it won't be that easy."

They watched the men set up the machine. Soon it began to work. It pumped a lot of the red water out of the river.

"It's working! That machine will do the job," Ben said. There was a smile on his face.

But there was no smile on Carol's face. "I don't think it will," she said.

"Why not?" Ben asked her.

"Look," she said. She pointed at the river. "The machine can't work fast enough. There's still a lot of red water left in the river. There's more and more of it."

Ben saw that she was right. "And it's changing the rest of the water that it touches," he said.

Ben went over to the man who spoke to them before. "Why don't you use two machines?" he asked him.

"Looks like we will have to," he said. "One isn't enough, that's for sure."

He told his men to set up a second machine. They did.

But still they couldn't get the red water out of the river fast enough.

Carol said to Ben, "Soon the river will be full of red water. All the way to the ocean!"

"I'm afraid you're right," Ben said.

Carol didn't say anything for a minute. She was thinking. Then she said, "I have an idea. I don't know if it will work or not but—" She looked at the two machines. Then she looked down at the river.

"I think I know how to stop that red water," she said.

She told her idea to Ben.

"That sounds like a great idea," he said. "I think it just might work!"

CHAPTER **5**

Gus

Ben and Carol went back to Ben's house.

Once there, Ben picked up the telephone in the kitchen. He called Jim Becker and told him about Carol's idea.

"I had thought of that already," Becker said. "That sort of thing can work very well in a laboratory. But how could you get it to work outside in a river?"

Ben told Carol what Jim had just said.

"Let me talk to him please," she said.

Ben gave her the telephone.

Carol explained her idea to Becker. She told him how she thought it could work outside.

"It does sound as if it might work," Becker said. "It's worth a try. I'll call some of the government people. I'll set up the experiment with them. I'll be in touch with you and Ben as soon as I can."

"That's fine," Carol said.

"One more thing. I want to thank you for your help," Becker said.

"You're welcome," Carol said. She put down the telephone. She told Ben what Jim Becker had said.

"I'll make some coffee for us," Ben said.

"Good," Carol said. "I sure would like a cup. I feel cold. The coffee will warm me up."

"It's almost November," Ben said, as he made a pot of coffee. "Winter will soon be here."

When the coffee was ready, Ben gave a cup of it to Carol.

A minute later, someone knocked on the door. Ben got up from the kitchen table. He went to the door and opened it.

"Hello there, Gus," he said. "Carol," he called out. "Your father is here. Come on in, Gus."

Carol came to the door. "Hello, Dad. Would you like a cup of coffee?"

"No, thank you," Gus Crane said. "I can't stay. I've been looking for King. Have either of you seen him around?"

Ben and Carol said they had not seen the dog.

Just then they heard a dog bark. The sound came from far away.

"Maybe that's King," Gus said. "I'll go and see if it is."

When Gus had left to look for King, Ben and Carol sat down again.

When Carol finished her coffee, she got up from the table. She went to the window and looked out.

"All the grass is dead down by the river," she said. "It used to be so green."

"Yes, I know it is," Ben said. "The red water has been sinking into the ground. Soon it will kill all the grass in the fields, too."

"And all the flowers, too," Carol said. Her voice sounded sad. "If we don't win our fight against that water."

"We will win," Ben said, "if your idea works. If it doesn't work—" He didn't finish his sentence.

"That looks like King down there," Carol said. "Why, it *is* King."

Ben got up and went to the window. He stood next to Carol. "Where is King going?"

Carol didn't answer. Instead, she ran to the door and opened it. "King!" she called to the dog. "Here, boy! Come here, King!"

King ran up to her. He began to bark.

"What's the matter, boy?" Carol said to the dog. "What is it?"

King ran away from her. He seemed to wait for her to come after him. When she didn't, he ran back to her. He began to bark again.

"I think he wants us to go with him," Ben said to Carol.

"Is that what you want, King?" Carol said.

King ran away from her again. He stopped and looked back at Carol. She went to him. King ran ahead of her. When Carol followed him, he kept on running.

Ben ran after both of them.

He caught up with Carol. "Maybe something is wrong."

"Something *must* be wrong," Carol said. "I've never seen King act like this before."

At last, King stopped next to the fence.

"Look," Carol said. "There is a big hole under the fence. King must have made that hole."

King began to bark again.

The dog crawled down into the hole. He came out on the other side of the fence. He ran to the river and barked.

It was then that Ben saw Carol's father. Gus was in the water. He couldn't seem to get out. He couldn't seem to walk.

Carol saw her father. "Oh, help him, Ben!" she called. "Save him!"

Ben acted at once. He crawled down into the hole that King had made. He came out on the other side of the fence.

He ran to the river.

He made a grab for Gus. He caught one of Gus' arms. He pulled him out of the water. He put him down on the ground.

Carol crawled down into the hole and then out of it. She ran up to her father.

Gus opened his eyes. "It was King. He—"

"I think I know what happened," Ben said. "King made that hole under the fence. He was going to get a drink of water from the river."

"I saw him," Gus whispered. "He was about to take a drink. I called his name. But he didn't come to me. I guess he thought it was all a game."

"You went under the fence after him," Ben said. "You wanted to save his life."

"Yes, I did," Gus said. "But I slipped and fell into the water. I couldn't get out. That water is too thick."

Gus closed his eyes again. "My legs hurt," he said. "They hurt me real bad."

Ben looked down at Gus' legs. "Get out of here, Carol," he said. He didn't want her to see her father's legs. "Go away!"

But Carol didn't go. She looked down at her father's legs.

They had turned into red jelly.

Even as Ben and Carol stood there, Gus' whole body began to turn into the same red jelly. Soon he was dead.

Carol screamed. She began to shake. She put her hands over her face and began to cry.

"Your father wanted to save the life of his friend," Ben said to her. "That was a very brave thing to do."

Carol could say nothing. She could only cry.

Ben wished there was something he could say to make her feel better. But he knew there wasn't anything.

He took Carol in his arms and held her close to him. It was all he could do for her.

And he knew it was not enough.

CHAPTER **6**

CAROL'S PLAN

Three days later, Ben drove Carol to her father's funeral.

When the funeral was over, he drove her back home to her farm.

When they got to Carol's house, she got out of the car. "Thank you," she said to Ben. She started to go inside.

"Wait," Ben said. "I'd like to talk to you if I may. Please."

Carol turned back to him. She looked at him. Her look seemed to say that there was nothing to talk about.

But Ben felt that he had to talk to her. "May I come inside with you?" he asked.

"If you want to," Carol said.

They went inside the house.

Ben sat down. "Carol," he began. "Can you try to tell me what is wrong?"

"You don't *know* what is wrong?" she said. "My father—"

"Your father is dead, Carol," Ben said. "But you're not."

Ben could tell that Carol was angry with him. It showed on her face. But he knew what he was doing. He had to try to make her understand.

He said, "I know you are hurt. I know how bad you feel. But I also know this. Your father wouldn't want you to give up. He would want you to live."

"I don't want to live," Carol said. "Not without him. I feel so alone."

"But you're not alone," Ben said.

She looked up at him. "What do you mean?"

"You're not alone," he said again. "Because *I'm* here with you."

Carol said, "You have been very kind to me. I know you only want to help me but—"

"Carol, think about this. I had a call from Jim Becker yesterday. He is going to send some men out here. They want to try the experiment that you told him about."

Carol shook her head from side to side. "No," she said. "I don't care about all that now."

Ben got to his feet. He walked across the room to Carol. He took her hands in his own. He lifted her to her feet and looked into her eyes.

"That red water killed your father," he said. "Don't you want to get even with it? Don't you want to fight it—because it killed your father?"

Carol looked away.

"Look at me," Ben said. "Answer me!"

"I—I don't know," Carol said at last.

"You *do* know," Ben said. "You're strong. You don't quit. I want you to fight back. Do it for your father."

Carol's face changed. Ben saw that she wasn't angry now.

"You're right," she said finally. "I *will* fight."

"Great!" Ben said. "I knew you wouldn't just give up. I knew you wouldn't quit. You're not that kind of person."

"I don't really know what kind of person I am," Carol said.

Ben said, "I know. You are very nice. Very brave. And very dear to me."

"Thank you, Ben. Thank you very much."

"It's *true*," Ben said, with a smile. "Now I think we had better talk about your experiment. Jim Becker said the men would be here today. I told him we would meet them at my house. Will you come over there with me?"

"Yes, I'll be there," Carol said. "As soon as I change my clothes."

Later, they drove to Ben's house. They found the men were already there.

Ben spoke to them. He told them who he was and who Carol was.

The men said they were from the electric company. "We were told to talk to Carol Crane," one of them said.

"I'm Carol Crane," Carol said.

"My name is Montoya. Al Montoya. They told us that you would tell us what to do," he said.

"Come with me, please," Carol said.

Montoya and his men followed her to a tall electric pole.

Carol pointed to the wires at the top of the pole. "We can get electricity from up there. But first you have to turn off the electricity up there for a while."

"Then what?" asked Montoya.

"Then you run a wire from up there down to the ground," Carol said. "Have you got some good strong wire?"

Montoya said they had some.

"Good," Carol said. "When you get it fixed up there, let me know."

Montoya and his men went to work. When they had finished, they came back to Carol.

"OK," she said. "That's fine. Now we have to run that wire down to the river."

She helped the men carry the heavy wire down to the river. It lay like a long black snake on the ground.

"Put the end of the wire into the water," Carol ordered the men.

They looked at her and then at each other. "What for?" they asked her.

"We have to get electricity into the water," she answered.

When the men had put the wire in the river, Carol told them what else to do. They must go back and turn on the electricity at the top of the pole.

When the men left, Carol asked Ben where the two machines were.

"They are gone," Ben said. "The machines just didn't work fast enough. And the men didn't have any more. So they gave up. They took the machines away."

"The men gave up?" Carol said. "Well, *we* won't give up, will we?"

Ben gave her a big smile. He pressed her hand. "No, we won't."

"The electricity is on," Montoya yelled.

"Now let's see what happens," Carol said to Ben. "Let's see if it works."

They walked down to the edge of the river.

Montoya and his men joined them. They all watched the river. They could see the wire run from the pole into the red water. The electricity was making the water give off sparks. The sparks flashed and cracked. There was a strong electric smell in the air. There was also the smell of gas.

Suddenly, one of the men gave a shout. "It's working!" he yelled. "The water is starting to dry up."

It was true. They could see the red water starting to dry up.

"The electricity does that," Carol said. "It breaks the water up. It turns it into a gas. I learned about that when I was in school. But I never thought knowing about it would be of any use to me."

In three hours, the river was almost all dry. There was only a little bit of red water left in it.

Suddenly, it began to rain.

"Oh, no!" Ben said.

When the rain hit the red water in the river, it turned into red water, too. Soon the river began to fill up with red water again.

"We have lost our fight," Carol said.

"Yes, I'm afraid we have," Ben said.

"What now?" Carol asked him.

"I just don't know," he answered. "I have no idea what to try next."

CHAPTER **7**

THE DAM

One week later, all the grass on Ben's farm was dead. So were the trees. When the wind blew, dirt flew everywhere.

All Ben's cows were dead. His chickens were dead also.

For many miles around, people did not have enough safe water to drink. They had to get it from other towns. The water from the other towns cost a lot of money.

Some people didn't have enough money to buy water. So some of them got sick.

The government helped the people. The government gave them free water. But there was never enough. Some people would steal the water that the government sent. Then they would sell it themselves at a very high cost.

The government also sent the army back. The army was ordered to build a dam near one end of the river. The dam would keep the red water away from the ocean. Some people said that the army should not build the dam. They said it might break.

But the army did build the dam.

Carol was one of the people who didn't want the dam.

She came with King to visit Ben one day. It was in early November.

She said, "Ben, I worry about that dam. The army put it up too fast. I don't think it is strong enough to hold back all that water."

"The government said it was OK," Ben said.

"Well, maybe it is. But I still worry."

Ben could see that Carol didn't look well. "Would you like a drink of water, Carol? I have a whole bottle full."

"No," Carol said. "I don't want a drink."

But Ben knew that she did. No one had enough water to drink. Not Ben. Not Carol. Not anyone. He went into the kitchen. He came back with a bottle of water and a glass. He filled the glass with water. He gave it to Carol. "Drink that," he said.

"Do you have more?" she asked him.

He shook his head. "Just a little."

"I don't want it," she said again. "But King does. May I give him a little bit of this water?"

"Sure," Ben said. He got a dish and Carol put the water in the dish. King drank the water.

"Now you drink the rest," Ben said to Carol. He could see in her eyes how much she needed a drink of water. Her hands were shaking as she took the glass from Ben. She was afraid she would drop it and spill the water.

"I remember when there was water enough for everyone," she said. "It seems like only yesterday. And now—"

"Try not to think about it," Ben said, a sad smile on his face.

Later, Ben said, "Let's take a walk. Do you want to?"

"OK. Where do you want to go?"

"Let's walk up on the hill behind my house."

They did. King went with them.

They stood on top of the hill and looked around. No matter where they looked, they saw the same thing. There was nothing but dry dirt all over. All the trees were dead. A few thin farm animals still walked around. The animals were looking for something to eat.

Many of the houses that they saw were empty. The people who lived in them had moved away.

"Maybe we should go away from here," Carol said. "Like so many others have."

"I hate to go," Ben said. "I don't really want to go. This is my home now."

"But there may be more trouble coming," Carol said. "The government said we should all move to the desert. There isn't any water in the desert. So the red water can't come there. They said we would be safe there."

"I know that," Ben said. "The government said they don't think they can stop the red water now."

"This could mean the end of our world," Carol said. "And the end of you and me."

Ben had been thinking the same thing. "Do you want to go to the desert?"

"Do you?" Carol asked him.

"We could go there together," Ben said.

They began to walk back down the hill. King ran along beside them.

"I think we should go to the desert," Carol said at last.

"Let's do this," Ben said. "Let's pack our clothes. We can take some bottles of water with us. We will just get in my car and drive away. When we feel like it, we stop."

"You make it sound like a vacation."

"We can call it a vacation."

"When will we go?" Carol asked.

"Tomorrow," Ben said.

"Tomorrow?" Carol looked at Ben. "I don't even want to think about tomorrow. I want to escape from tomorrow. I'm afraid of it."

"But we have to face it," Ben said.

"Yes, I know we do."

They came to the fence by the side of the river. They walked along beside it until they came to the dam.

"The water is pretty high behind the dam," Ben said.

"How I hate that red water," Carol said.

She didn't say anything more.

Ben looked at her. He knew what she was thinking about. She was thinking about her father.

Ben took her hand as they walked along without saying anything.

They were almost past the dam when Carol suddenly stopped.

"What is it?" Ben asked her. "Is something wrong?"

"I'm not sure," Carol said. She was looking at the dam. "Look up there, Ben." She pointed to a place near the top of the dam.

"I don't see— Wait a minute! Is that a—?"

"It's a crack in the dam," Carol said. "You can see where the water is coming through the crack. It's running down the side of the dam over there. Can you see it?"

"Yes," Ben said, "I can see it." He pressed Carol's hand without knowing that he did so. Let's get out of here."

They started back toward Ben's house as fast as they could.

"I told you that dam was weak," Carol said, looking back at it.

Suddenly, they heard a loud noise.

"What was that noise?" Carol asked.

Ben knew she was afraid. "It's the dam," he told her. "It's going to break because of that crack. Run for it!"

Together they began to run toward Ben's house. King ran with them.

"Let's get my bottle of safe water," Ben said as they ran. "Then we can take my car and drive to the desert."

At last they got to Ben's house. They both ran inside. So did King.

"Let me sit down for a minute," Carol said. "I feel weak." Her heart was pounding.

"No," Ben said to her. "We have to get out of here—fast. The dam might break any minute now. Come on!"

He picked up the bottle of water from the table. It was all the safe water he had.

He started toward the front door with Carol beside him.

"If the dam breaks, we had better not be here to see it happen," Ben said.

"Where's King?" Carol said. She looked around. The dog was gone.

"King!" she called out.

"Maybe he went into the kitchen," Ben said.

Just then King began to bark. Ben and Carol couldn't see the dog but they could hear him.

"He must be in the kitchen," Ben said. "King!" he yelled.

King made a noise that wasn't a bark. It was more like a scream. He ran into the living room from the kitchen. He ran over to Carol.

Suddenly, a strange man came out of Ben's kitchen. In his hand, he held a gun.

"Don't move," he said. "And keep that dog away from me. If you don't, I'll kick him again." He pointed the gun at Carol and Ben.

"Who are you? How did you get in here?" Ben asked the man.

"I broke a window in the kitchen and climbed in," the man said.

"Why?" Carol asked. "What do you want?"

"I want money," the man said. "Give it to me now. If you don't, I'll kill you both."

"We have to get out of here," Ben shouted. "The dam is going to break."

"Stay where you are," the man said. "No one is going anywhere."

CHAPTER 8

THE MAN WITH THE GUN

"Give me your money!" the man yelled, waving his gun.

"I don't have any money with me," Carol told the man.

He looked at Ben. "What about you? Have you got any money?"

"Yes," Ben said. "I have some. Put that gun away and I'll get it."

"Get it," the man said. "I'll keep the gun."

Ben thought that the man was afraid of something. The gun in the man's hand shook. He acted, Ben thought, as if he had never held a gun before.

"The money is in my desk over there," Ben said. He started to walk toward the desk.

"You come over here," the man said to Carol. "Stand next to me."

Carol didn't move.

"Did you hear what I said?" the man yelled. *"Come over here!"*

Carol went and stood next to the man. He grabbed her right arm.

"Don't try any tricks," he said to Ben. "If you do, she will get hurt. Got that?"

"I understand," Ben said.

When he got to his desk, Ben took the money out of it.

When the man saw the money, he said, "Throw it on the floor."

Ben did as he was told.

King ran to the money on the floor. He picked it up in his teeth.

"King," Carol said. "Put that money down. This isn't a game."

King looked up at Carol. She told him a second time to drop the money. He did. Then he began to bark.

"Stop that noise!" the man yelled at King. Then he yelled at Carol. "Make that dog stop that noise!"

"King," Carol said. *"Stop it!"*

King stopped.

The man let Carol go. He picked up the money. He put it in his pocket.

"What are you going to do with that money?" Ben asked the man.

"What do you care?" the man said. He began to move toward the door.

"I just wondered," Ben said. "You don't look like the kind of man who would steal."

The man's face changed. He looked very sad. "I'm not," he said. "I never did anything like this before."

"I thought so," Ben said.

"But I had to have some money," the man said. "My family needs water. We don't have any left. We have to buy some. I didn't have any money to buy water."

Ben took a step toward the man. The man didn't see him move. Ben took another step.

The man said, "We just had a baby girl. But the baby will die if we don't give her enough water. We must have water."

"What about the free water the government gives away?" Carol said. "Didn't you get any?"

"We got some at first," the man said. "But the government can't send us any water now. They ran out of water four days ago."

Ben and Carol knew that what the man said was true.

"I'm sorry," the man said. "But I just had to do this. Please try to understand."

"Put down that gun," Ben said.

The man didn't put the gun down. He pointed it at Ben. "Don't try any tricks," he said. "I'll shoot you if I have to."

He turned. He was about to run for the door.

But King was in his way. The big dog barked once and jumped at the man. The gun flew out of the man's hand as he fell over on his back.

"Good dog, King!" said Carol.

"Get his gun, Carol!" Ben yelled. He grabbed the man. He made him get to his feet.

"Did you get the gun?" he asked Carol.

"Yes," she said.

"Give it to me."

Carol gave the gun to him.

"Let me go," the man said. "Please let me go. If you let me go, I'll give you back your money."

"Carol, call the police," Ben said. To the man, he said, "I'm sorry for you and your family. But you could have killed us. If I let you go, you will probably try this again. Next time, you might kill someone."

Carol called the police. She told Ben that the police said they couldn't come.

"Why not?" Ben wanted to know.

"They told me to get out of here," Carol said.

"They said the dam was going to break. They said if we stay here, we would be killed."

"The dam! I almost forgot!" Ben said. He was looking at Carol. He didn't see the man move toward the door.

The man opened the door and ran out of the house.

"Ben!" Carol called out. "He got away!"

"Let him go," Ben said. "We have more important things to worry about now. Let's get out of here."

They left the house with King. Ben left the gun behind him.

"Oh, it's very cold now," Carol said. "It wasn't this cold before. The sun is gone."

"Take my coat," Ben said. He gave it to her and she put it on. "It looks like it's going to rain again," he said.

"If it does, that will be the end," Carol said. "Come on. My car is over there."

But before they could make a move, there was a loud noise.

The dam broke with a roar. Red water came rushing out.

"Run!" Ben yelled.

They ran toward Ben's car.

"Look," Carol said. "There's the man that wanted to rob us."

Red water rushed toward Ben's house like a moving wall of jelly. The man was in its way. He screamed. The water touched him. It turned him into red jelly just like itself.

"Quick!" Ben said to Carol. "We have to get to the car."

"But we can't!" Carol said. "The water is almost at the car already. It's coming this way!"

"Run back the other way!" Ben yelled. *"Come on! Run!"*

Together they ran as the water came rushing toward them.

CHAPTER **9**

WINTER COMES

Ben and Carol ran as fast as they could. So did King.

The water was not far behind them. It ran all over the ground, covering everything in its way.

"Let's climb that hill!" Ben said. He pointed to the hill they had climbed before. "Maybe the water won't get to the top of the hill."

"Wait!" Carol called out to him. "Look! It's King! Some of the red water splashed on his legs! I have to save him."

She ran back to King. But she was too late to save him. King's legs had become red jelly.

He looked up at Carol. He gave one soft bark. Then his whole body turned into jelly. The water covered him up.

Carol ran back to Ben. "I couldn't save him," she said. "Oh, poor King!"

The red water was moving fast. It would reach them in another few seconds.

"Come on, Carol!" Ben yelled. "Let's make a run for it!"

They ran to the bottom of the hill. They began to climb it. But half-way up the hill, Ben fell down.

"I can't go on," he told Carol. "I think I broke my ankle. You had better go on alone."

"No," said Carol. "I won't leave you."

Carol put her arm around Ben. She put his arm over her shoulder. She helped him climb the hill. At last, they got to the top of the hill.

They looked down at the water. It was all over. The ground was covered with it. It looked like a big lake of blood.

"I did that," Ben said.

"What do you mean?"

"Jim Becker and I made the first little bit of that red water," Ben said. "We are the ones who made all this trouble."

Ben thought Carol would be surprised and angry. But she showed no feeling. They looked at each other without speaking. At last Ben said, "You knew it all along, didn't you?"

"Yes," Carol said. "When you said you worked at that laboratory, I had a feeling. But I know it was just an experiment. You didn't mean to make all this happen."

"All this because of an experiment," Ben said, hanging his head.

Below them, the water kept coming up the hill. Soon it was very close to where they stood.

Both Carol and Ben watched the water. They both knew that they were trapped on the hill. If the water kept coming . . . They didn't want to think about what would happen to them.

Ben's broken ankle hurt him. He sat down. Carol sat down beside him. Ben put his arm around her.

"It's very cold," Carol said. She looked up at the sky. "It looks like it's going to rain again."

"We will never get out of here if it rains," Ben said. "More rain means more red water. It will cover this whole hill."

Carol looked down at the red water. "Then this is the end," she said. "Oh, Ben, I didn't want it to end like this."

"Maybe it won't rain after all," Ben said. He wanted to make Carol feel better. "Maybe we will be safe here." But he didn't really believe it. Carol didn't either.

"Look at your house," Carol said. "All you can see of it is the roof. You can't see your car at all. It's under the red water."

Ben looked down at the roof of his house. That house—his land—all gone. His dream of a new life was gone with it.

Just then, Carol felt a drop of rain hit her face. "Rain," she said in a low voice.

They knew that there was nothing they could do. They were trapped on top of the hill.

All they could do was wait. Wait until the red water reached them and turned them to jelly.

They sat without speaking.

Then Ben saw something white on Carol's face. "Snow," he said. "The rain has turned to snow. It's snowing . . ."

"What does it matter?" Carol said. "Rain or snow. It's all water. And when the snow touches the red water, it will turn into red water, too."

The air turned very cold. Winter had come. They held each other close to keep warm as they watched the snow fall into the red water.

"I didn't want it to end like this either," Ben said to Carol. "I had hoped that—" He didn't finish his sentence. He saw that something was happening to the red water. It was turning to ice in the cold November air.

Ben began to wonder about the ice. About how it was different from water. But he was afraid to tell Carol what he was thinking. He might be wrong. If he told her, Carol would begin to hope again. If he was wrong, her new hope would soon die—as they would die with it.

"Ben," Carol said, looking at him. "What is it? What's on your mind?"

"Nothing," Ben said.

"Please, Ben. What is it?"

Ben told her. "The cold air is turning the red water into ice," he said. "Ice is different from water in many ways. I was just thinking that maybe the red ice will be different from the red water, too."

"And if it is?"

"And if it is, then maybe it—Wait! Look! I was right!" He pointed to the red water all around them. It was turning to ice. But that was not all.

As the red water turned to ice, it suddenly began to crack into little pieces. The wind began to blow. All the tiny pieces of ice broke again until each piece was like dust. And then it was gone.

Ben and Carol stood there, watching. They couldn't believe their eyes. As fast as the red water had formed, it was now going away just as fast. A few hours later, all the red ice was gone. There wasn't a sign of it in the air or on the ground.

"What happened to it?" Carol asked Ben. "I don't understand what happened to it."

"I don't either," Ben said. "But I think it had something to do with the cold. The cold destroyed the red water by turning it to ice.

Remember, that the red water wasn't like real water. It didn't act like real water at all. And the red ice didn't act like real ice either."

"So now it's all over," Carol said.

"Yes," Ben said. "We are safe. But it isn't all over yet."

"What do you mean?"

"I mean that we still must face tomorrow," Ben said. "So much has happened. Your father. My farm . . . I remember that you said you wanted to escape from tomorrow. Do you still want to?"

"Not now," Carol said. She stood up. "Let's go back down and start life all over again."

"Together?" Ben said.

"Yes, together," Carol answered. "Come on. I'll help you."

Ben put his arm over Carol's shoulder. She put her arm around him. She helped him climb down the hill.

When they got to the bottom of the hill, the snow had stopped.

Minutes later, the sun came out. It seemed to smile down on the two of them.